For Eliza —
To a fellow writer.
Susan Hawkins

Tina Christina Sestina

A Northwoods Adventure

Susan Hawkinson

Illustrated by Anna Cain

BLUEWATERS PRESS

Printed in the United States of America

First Edition, 2013

ISBN 978-0-9898444-0-6

Bluewaters Press
Box 246
Grand Rapids, MN 55744

susanondoan@gmail.com

Preface

Have you ever heard of a troubadour? If you haven't, they were poets, musicians, and often knights, who lived between 1100 and 1350 A.D. Troubadours traveled from castle to castle, reciting their poetry.

One of these troubadours invented a new form for a poem. He called it a *sestina*. The first six stanzas of the sestina each have six lines. The seventh stanza has three lines. Then it gets complicated. Each sestina has six rotating end-words. In the first sestina in the story about Tina Christina Sestina, the rotating end-words are *sister, closet, perimeter, skirt, figure,* and *girl.* You will see that some form of the six words appears in different orders at the ends of the lines in each of the six stanzas. The word *skirt,* for example, appears as *skirt, skirts, hoopskirt,* and *skirted.* In the seventh stanza, all six end-words are used within the three lines. Three of them appear any place in the lines while three appear at the end of the three lines. The end-words change with each new sestina. There are sixteen sestinas in this story. I have taken some liberties with the original form of the sestina. I haven't followed the rules perfectly.

Writing a sestina is like entering a labyrinth. You get to the end of the line, and it can feel like a dead end until the end-word becomes a door swung open by a new thought. And this new thought sometimes starts you in a direction that you hadn't even considered. One day I unlatched the door to an unfamiliar world when Tina Christina appeared on my computer screen. In some ways, she was me at eleven.

Let me tell you about my eleven-year-old self. I grew up, during the 1950s, in northern Minnesota about one hundred miles south of the Canadian border in the small town of Grand Rapids. My family lived on Fourth Avenue in a neighborhood full of young children. The Fourth Avenue gang of kids usually played in the big backyards that ran from our back doors all the way down to the shores of Hale Lake. But some days our mothers packed peanut butter and jelly sandwiches, filled our metal canteens with water, and let us go off to Big Pine.

Big Pine is what we called the woods on the north side of Hale Lake where nobody lived and the forest seemed to go on for miles. The way we got there was by walking down Fourth Avenue, crossing Hagmans' backyard, and passing between two 80-foot-tall white pines. Then we followed a footpath to the ridge trail that ran high above Hale Lake.

We made a point of leaving our neighborhood by passing between the two big white pines as we entered the forest. Somehow we knew that this ritual of passing between the two pines allowed us to move into a different place where time stands still. That is where our real adventures began.

Now take a deep breath and read *Tina Christina Sestina* slowly, so you don't get lost in the labyrinth of words. Make sure the end-words swing wide open.

Acknowledgments

Thanks to these individuals for reading as well as listening to *Tina Christina Sestina*. She is someone I have come to understand more clearly because of each of you: Teresa Alto, Elizabeth Blair, Stan Cronister, Connie Daigle and past students, Annie Erickson, Jan Ferraro, Nancy Mike-Johnson and her 2012-2013 fourth grade class, Loree Miltich, Doug and Sylvia Olney, and my family.

Christened for her aunt, her mother's sister,
Christina wore the hoopskirt from the closet.
It gave her a broader perimeter
than would a sleek, straight skirt,
which clung and showed her figure.
Christina was not an average girl.

Dress-up was the fame game of the girls
she knew at school – in particular, two sisters,
whose stunning curves gave them gorgeous figures.
A fantastic number of outfits filled their closet:
Woolen, crepe, silk, and linen, straight skirts
with matching sweaters. Around the perimeter

of the closet were their scarves and pearls. "A perimeter
of scarves and pearls," mused the namesake girl
as she walked to school one morning in her hoopskirt.
Her pearls – snails, crawfish claws, and turtle shell – both sisters
stroked, then held, that night inside her closet
where Aunt Tina's lamp – a night light – lit each figure.

The rub came when the gorgeous sisters figured
they could barter their vast perimeter
of scarves and pearls for a closet
shelf of snails and crawfish claws plus the namesake girl's
single turtle shell. The sisters
asked to trade that very day, but Christina skirted

the offer. "Scarves and pearls are worn with straight skirts.
I wear a hoopskirt. I cut a broader figure.
The summer camp of my mother's sister
isn't located on the vogue perimeter
but on the shores of Big Lake Water," explained the namesake girl.
"Her closet

is cached in a tall pine." "Take us to see this tree-hung closet,"
begged the sisters, who wore their linen straight skirts.
"I'll ask if we can visit," said the namesake girl.
Jumping up and down, jiggling their figures,
they expanded their perimeters
and hurried home. Exuberant were the sisters.

Tina Christina figured perimeters
would shift sharply for these shapely girls
whose sister skirts ruled their walk-in closet.

Not till June would Christina travel with the sisters
to the water where waves daily cast their spray
upon the rocky shore. High above, the tree-hung closet
swung in fluctuating breezes
as Aunt Tina wrote her niece, "To mark the trail, I'll build cairns.
Track these stacked stones for one night and two full days."

"One night and two full days!
Each way! And then we stay?" complained the sisters.
Christina felt in her soles the pull of her aunt's cairns
and in her heart relentless yearning for the spray.
In the fine hairs on her arms the fickle breeze.
In her ears the creaking tree song from the closet.

The two girls' curiosity about the closet
made them forget one night and two full days.
Like Christina, they began to feel the breeze
and knew they had to go. The gorgeous-figured sisters
wondered what to take along. "Our lipstick and our hairspray?
Our scarves, our real-deal pearls, our tight skirts?" The cairns

called to the sisters who'd never seen a cairn.
Nor had they seen a closet
rock above the spray.
"Christina, our father won't let us go for days and days!"
"My aunt'll send an invitation," Christina told the sisters,
"printed on birchbark and posted on the breeze.

It'll arrive through an open window. The breeze
is much faster than post office speed. She'll explain the cairns
will keep us on the trail." "Okay," said the sisters,
who corked their curiosity about the closet.
For days
the spray-

spewn shore vanished from their minds as they sprayed
their hair and dressed for school. But when spring breezes
started blowing daily,
the girls exclaimed, "We've found a cairn!
Can Aunt Tina's closet
be that far away?" The sisters

longed for what wasn't in their closet
and restacked Aunt Tina's cairn after school each day.
"This is a breeze," said the sisters. Far away, the three smelled the spray.

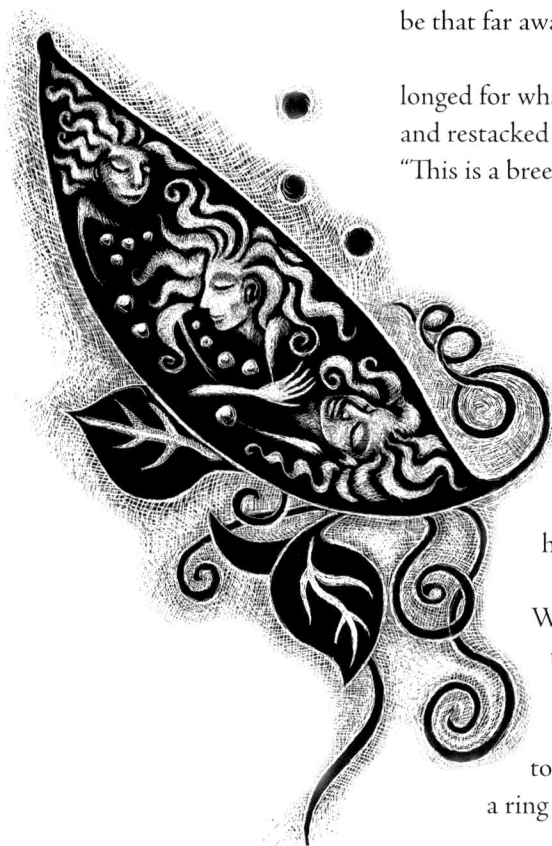

The girls took their prized possessions:
    Tina Christina, her snails, crawfish claws, and turtle shell;
        the sisters, their scarves and real-deal pearls.
        The gorgeous-figured sisters wore their straight, stretch
        skirts. Christina wore her hoopskirt, swung Aunt Tina's lamp,
    her night light, toward the growing dark.

When it became too dark
    to find the trail, the three girls set their prized possessions
        beneath a stand of pines and hung Aunt Tina's lamp
        to see. Christina strung her snails, claws, and turtle shell
        together as a wind chime while the sisters stretched
    a ring of scarves around the trees. Their real-deal pearls

began to shine like stars upon their sweaters. "Our pearls,"
said the sisters, "have never glowed in the dark."
"It's never dark enough at home," said Christina as she stretched
her sore arms and rested on her pack. "Here our prized possessions
can become more than the mere shells
of what they are at home. Now rub Aunt Tina's lamp

and watch the lamp
turn iridescent like your pearls."
Tina Christina listened to her turtle shell
chime softly in the dark.
"That's why we prize our best possessions.
They help us stretch

who we are through our imagination." Stretching
out beneath the white pines and the lamp,
the three girls listened to the whispering wind: "Possess
yourselves, not your possessions." Cried the real-deal pearls,
"But some of us are worth possessing." In the dark,
the three girls nestled like three peas unshelled

in a green pod and watched the faint half-shell
of moon move through the silent pines, stretching
eighty feet above them. The dark
night blew out Aunt Tina's lamp
and dulled the real-deal pearls.
And the girls went to sleep with their possessions.

When dawn's lamp lit up the morning sky, the sisters' pearls
were only pearls. The three girls stretched and talked about the dark,
packing their possessions while the wind still chimed the shell.

The sisters found the stacked stones just beyond two pines,
as the three traveled single file on a deer trail. When the air
flared out like wings and bore them swiftly over ground,
the sisters knew they'd reach the rocky spray-spewn shore
of the big water whose name
they didn't know. The sisters had to trust the namesake girl.

That afternoon the three girls
stopped beneath the white pines
when the name-
sake girl exclaimed, "Flying fish are coasting on the air
currents high above us near Big Lake Water's shore!"
Lying on their packs on the ground,

the sisters hooked their lines with pearls. Against a sky blue background
Christina and the fame-game girls
watched a school of fish cascade through the trees above the shore.
From the crowns of the tall pines
throughout their lower limbs, flying fish filled the air,
cavorting pine to pine. Casting lines into the name-

less sea of trees, the girls caught more than they could eat. The namesake girl, lifting her backpack off the ground,
breathed in the sweet moist air,
and soon the three girls
reached Aunt Tina's summer camp below the tall pines
above the rocky shore.

Amidst the shore-
borne rocks and driftwood, a great blue heron fished. The namesake girl tossed a pine-
cone that she'd picked up off the ground
and called out to her long-necked friend, "The town girls
are in camp. Tell Aunt Tina." After two days of fresh air,

the girls fell asleep, heads resting on their packs. The air
churned up along Big Lake Water's shore
and fanned the fire while the girls
slept on for hours. Sound asleep, the namesake girl talked with her aunt who ground
the herbs and cornmeal for a fish fry beneath her stand of pines.

Tina Christina and the sisters found safe ground
beneath the pines above the shore. "Now you know," said the namesake girl,
"about the wild life in the open air."

The next day before daylight Aunt Tina lit a fire
and filled her teapot with dried herbs and Big Lake Water
to brew her morning tea. She listened to the wind
sing among the trees and to her teapot whistle
while the girls whispered to each other in their sleep.
"All three are wading in a creek bed in their dream,"

thought Aunt Tina as she looked into the flames. "These dreams" –
she sipped her tea and stirred the fire –
"will be their teachers, the wild life they'll meet in sleep."
Teapot disturbed her reverie: "More water."
Its high-pitched whistle
woke the girls, who mistook it for the wind

blowing through their hair. Talking to the wind,
they complained, "We want to sleep and dream
about the creek." Whistling
Teapot disagreed. "Get up, you lazy girls. The fire's
almost out, and I'm nearly out of water.
Don't fall back to sleep."

Aunt Tina's teapot continued whistling to the sleepy
girls. "Fan the fire. Shield it from the wind.
Take the trail to the shore, and get more Big Lake Water.
It's almost daybreak. Let go of your sweet dreams
before the fire
gives up its flame and I can't whistle."

"Will you teach us how to whistle?"
asked the sisters. "Otherwise we'd rather sleep."
"Teapot will teach you if you rebuild the fire
and get more water," said South Wind.
"Then our life will be the dream,"
said the sisters, rolling out of bed to fetch the water.

"Take a pan from the pan tree on your way for water,"
said Aunt Tina as the sisters tried to whistle.
Forgotten was their shared creek dream
along with their deep sleep.
On the rocky shores below the camp, South Wind
roused the waves for easy water while the fire

nearly went to sleep. "Hurry with the water," South Wind
cried. "You can't recall your dreams
or learn to whistle without both fire and water."

Dreams can take us places
hidden during daylight hours.
In your shared dream you cool your tired feet
in a creek
not far from here," said Tina Christina's aunt.
"You know about this creek?" asked the fame-game girls.

Aunt Tina sipped her tea and said, "Girls,
when I look into the fire, I see places
in other people's dreams." Aunt
Tina paused, looking at the sisters and her niece. "In the hours
between evening dark and daybreak, you'll reach your dream creek
guided solely by your feet.

Your feet
will be your daylight eyes." The fame-game girls
wondered more and more about their dream creek.
They felt pulled toward this hidden place.
"Gaze into our
fire," said Aunt

Tina. "What do you see?" Aunt
Tina looked directly at Christina. "Our bare feet
are dangling in the cool water of our
creek," said the namesake girl.
"Look again into the fire. You'll see more places
to help you find your dream creek."

Aunt Tina left her niece to conjure up the creek,
while she taught the sisters how to build a fire. "Aunt
Tina, this place
points my feet
upstream," called out the namesake girl.
Hour

by slow hour,
Christina saw the dream creek
while her girl-
friends gathered herbs and berries with Aunt
Tina. Crouching on their hands and feet,
they learned to find herbs by themselves in secret places.

"We'll travel to the dream creek without Aunt Tina. Our feet
will be our guides," murmured Christina to the girls.
"The place we find tonight will be ours all hours."

That night the three attached their prized possessions to their packs:
Christina, her crawfish claws, turtle shell, and snails;
the sisters, their real-deal pearls and scarves.
Aunt Tina stood on the ridge above the shore and let them go.
"You know the creek will flow
into Big Lake Water. You'll hear the creek before you see it.

Before daybreak, you need to reach it."
The girls heaved their backpacks
onto their shoulders. "Are you sure we'll hear the creek flow?"
asked the sisters. "We'll move slow like snails,"
replied the namesake girl. "I'll go
first. Now tie your scarves

together. I'll tie the string of scarves
around my waist, and you two tie it
to each of yours. Then we can safely go
along the ridge above the shore." After tightening her pack
straps, Tina Christina kept a snail's
pace as she listened for the creek flow.

The three girls walked and walked and did not hear the flow
of water. The string of scarves
flapped in the breeze and the snails
and crawfish claws chimed with the turtle shell. "It's
further than I thought," said Christina, repositioning her pack.
"How far do we dare go

without returning?" asked the sisters. "We'll go,"
said Christina, "until we hear the creek flow."
The sisters were tired of their packs.
The string of scarves
collapsed. But not long after that, the night lost its
dark hold on Earth. The crawfish claws and snails

quit chiming with the turtle shell. Their snail's
pace paused momentarily. There wasn't far to go.
The gorgeous-figured sisters said to the namesake girl, "It
sounds like our dream creek flowing
into Big Lake Water!" The string of scarves
untied themselves. The girls threw off their packs.

"Leave your packs," said Christina. "Go sit by the creek." The scarves
blew in the breeze above the water while its
fast flow rinsed the turtle shell, the pearls, the crawfish claws, and snails.

The girls waited to hear what their creek would say.
It gurgled up around six stepping stones
to speak. "Lie down
now on my banks
and sleep. Close your eyes
before day breaks the dark."

The girls were used to sleeping in the dark
and wondered, "Will sleep come when it gets light?" But saying
anything seemed impolite. They closed their eyes
as dawn streaked the sky and settled on the stones.
Rather late the three girls awakened on the creek bank.
Tina Christina looked down-

stream and saw marsh marigolds beyond a downed
jack pine, dark
and decomposing on the bank.
Christina said
to the sisters, "Look beyond the fallen pine and stepping stones."
Bright-eyed,

the namesake girl focused her friends' eyes
on the cups of gold set on saucers of green leaves down
beyond the stones.
The three girls leaped into the dark
pool of moving water, saying
nothing. Wading between the creek banks,

the girls touched one bank
and then the other as they eyed
the new world all around them. "Say,"
said the sisters, "let's pluck a cup of gold to carry home." Down-
stream wound a thousand marigolds, lost in the distant dark.
Six Stepping Stones

cried out, "Don't pluck the cup. Look up. Step on my stones.
Rainbows will flow into the cups. The banks
will glow a brilliant gold." The sisters' dark
green eyes
grew large in size, standing on the stones, looking up and down.
Saying,

"Jump!" in unison, the three leaped down
once more from the bank into the dark
creek water. "I say your eyes are opened," said Six Stepping Stones.

The three girls waded in the water all day long
and watched their shadows
play on the gold banks of the creek as the sun swung
in slow motion across the dome of sky.
Lost in thought,
the three walked upstream to find the creek source.

Where the creek bed narrowed, the Source
called out to the sisters. "What is it that you long
for?" The question didn't take much thought.
The gorgeous-figured sisters knew beyond the shadow
of a doubt. The sky
was turning purple when the sisters swung

their arms and said, "More scarves and pearls." By then the sun had swung
its bright lamp into the crowns of trees. Said the Source,
"More is only more. It will never be enough." Sky
nodded in agreement. Along
the narrow creek bed, shadows
swiftly gathered according to their height. The sisters thought

about *enough* and *more* and also thought
about their scarves and pearls as the sun swung
out of sight. Several of the shadows
drew near to hear the Source
when it spoke once more to the girls." You must be going. A long
return trip lies ahead, and the sky

is almost dark." The three girls looked at the sky
as a great horned owl flew overhead and hooted. Thought
the sisters, "Could it sink its talons in our scalps, such a long
way from Aunt Tina?" Christina swung
her arms around the girls as they raced from the creek source
to the six stepping stones. The shadows

ran beside the three. The taller shadows
coldly curled around their elbows. Sky
put on her summer constellations, the source
of light for the girls' safe traveling. Thought
each of the two sisters who spoke as one, "We've swung
ourselves back to the six stepping stones after a long

walk up the creek!" For a long time the sisters' choice swung
back and forth from *enough* to *more*. They thought about the creek source
as they stood beneath the sky among the shadows.

When midnight struck on the celestial clock, the
dream creek gurgled softly to the girls, "Find a stone
on which to lay your head. Sleep until you dream again. Then wake."
The gorgeous-figured sisters and the namesake girl
lay on their backs on the creek bank and closed their eyes
while tiny dots of starlight burst into a brilliant night.

The same great horned owl, hunting late that night,
hovered above the sleeping girls. Owl listened to the
song of the evening breezes while a sky of starry eyes
kept careful watch and the gemstones
in Orion's belt burned bright. The namesake girl
dreamed herself awake,

startled by the fan of air above her. "Awake,
Miss Namesake? Hoo, hoo are you?" asked Owl. The night
had camouflaged the creature as he landed near the girl.
"I'm going to fly you to the
moon where you can see the dreams from your stone
sleep play on the stage of the night sky. Like stars, your eyes

will leap, your heart will shine. Now open the eyes
of the two sisters. We must be wide-awake
to take this ride. Gather the three stones
you slept on. Stack them three stones high. When night
has faded into dawn, the
stones will balance on the point of your return. Girls,

hang on tight for the ride." The girls
lassoed the owl with the sisters' string of scarves. Their eyes
rimmed with mystery, they climbed onto the
stones and took a reckless leap to reach the bird. Awake
to possibility, the three embraced the night
and left behind the creek and the stacked stones.

Beneath the soaring girls, the stacked stones
shrunk to miniatures, then disappeared. Said Owl, "Girls,
tonight
is a full moon." The girls rubbed their eyes,
awakened,
saw the moonlight. It was the

first time the sisters and the namesake girl felt wide-awake
in their shared dream. Said Owl to the bright-eyed girls, "Tonight,
reach for the moon! You dared to leap from three stacked stones."

*A*board Owl and beneath the moon,
the irises in the girls' eyes bloomed in their shared dream. They saw a
bioluminescent light cast their bones
in violet while a red halo drafted in their
wake. Owl exclaimed, "A flying saucer without a cup!
The Martians drink their tea straight from the pot!"

Just then a Martian teapot
poured by them on their all-night flight to the moon,
and the three girls stuck Aunt Tina's cups
into the teapot's stream of Martian tea. A
wand of lightning struck the three girls on their crowns. Their
bodies shook with thunder right to their violet bones.

In the featherbed aboard the bird, their bones
sunk into the lofty down and the Martian teapot
poured them all another cup. Their
night flight to the moon
passed pleasantly until a
comet caught its tail in their three cups,

and hiccuped, breaking all three cups
into strands of bone-
bright light. Their hair curled and uncurled. A
burst of arctic air froze the Martian teapot's
spout. Owl said, "Goodbye, girls. Mr. Moon
Man is waiting for you. There,

there.
Everything is going to be all right. Your cups
will pull themselves together before you reach Mr. Moon.
Don't fall asleep. Be night owls." Bone-
tired, they waved goodbye to Owl and the Martian teapot
before they saw Mr. Moon Man fly high on a

trapeze. "A one ring circus on a
big screen!" the awestruck sisters shouted to their
guides. The Martian teapot
squeaked out a whistle. Owl was nowhere to be seen. Cupping
bone-
cold hands around their mouths, the three girls called out to Moon

Man. "Mr. Moon Man, we're chilled to the bone!"
"They're ch-chilled to the bone!" a shivering Martian teapot
agreed. "And I have no m-m-more c-c-cups of t-e-a!"

$\mathcal{M}$r. Moon Man dropped
a hooked line in front of them
as he swung by on his trapeze. The fame-game
and namesake girls each grabbed a hook
in their shared dream, whirling almost beyond the pull
of gravity. Hanging

onto her hook, Christina shouted to the girls, "Hang
on to me! Hang on for this wild ride!" And they didn't drop
each other's hands until the pull
of Mr. Moon Man whirled them back. Talking to themselves
and to the stars around them, they shouted out, "We're hooked!"
And then the fame-game

girls dropped their pearls into the starry night. "Now we're game
for anything!" The three watched Mr. Moon Man hang
by a wire, hook
his arms through theirs, and drop
them
one by one onto his bar. The pull

of this wild world astonished the two girls. Pulling
Tina Christina even closer, the fame-game
girls hugged the namesake girl as she sat between them.
Still hanging
onto Mr. Moon Man, Christina and the sisters dropped
their hooks

and watched each hook
fly out beyond the pull
of gravity. In their amazement the three dropped
off to sleep, rocked by Mr. Moon on his trapeze. The fame-game
girls and Christina, hanging
onto Mr. Moon Man, knew he wouldn't leave them.

Mr. Moon watched over them
and kept his two arms, plus a third pulled from his pocket, hooked
through theirs. Still hanging
on his wire, he pulled
a sheet of clouds across Christina and the fame-game
girls, who had, at an early hour for the Moon Man, dropped

into a deep sleep. The pull of something wild had hooked the fame-game
girls, kept them hanging,
while another dream dropped into all of them.

"Before dawn you'll slide down a wire
back to Earth,"
said Mr. Moon Man to the three girls in their dream.
"Then you can keep your two feet grounded
or on moonlit nights
fly up again to see

me." Mr. Moon Man could see
their dream eyes moving rapidly. "Wire
me a sign on those nights
when Owl lands on Earth's
bright ground.
He'll fly with you to the dream

world. Dream
girls, fly up again to see
me. The ground
will shrink beneath you. When you reach the wire,
send Owl back to Earth
and swing with me all night

on my trapeze." Mr. Moon Man woke the three girls late that night
in the middle of their dream,
and the girls slid back to Earth –
a twirling top of continents and seas.
They meandered on the wire
toward solid ground

until the ground
came up to meet them. The night
rewound the wire
and returned it to Mr. Moon Man in their dream.
"We've seen,"
said Christina, sprawled on a slightly spinning berm of Earth,

"the strangest things on and beyond this Earth."
More grounded
than before, the sisters enthusiastically agreed, "We see
now there's a lot that we don't see." The night
fled as dawn flung her rosy arms across the sky. Their dream
faded like a painting hung in too much light. Wired

and wide-awake on the ground, they spoke more about their dreams
and the strange nights they'd seen,
riding on the owl and sliding down the wire back to Earth.

*B*ack on Earth again
the girls walked along the shore of Big Lake Water
where the creek flowed past the shore
and disappeared into the waves.
Their packs seemed lighter
when they started off for home.

Tina Christina's aunt met them home-
bound when they passed her camp again.
"Come up and see my closet," said Aunt Tina. Light-
heartedly, the three climbed to the ridge above the water
and sat down around the fire. The waves
were lapping gently on the shore.

"Your dreams are large," said Aunt Tina, eyes on the far shore.
"I see it in your blooming irises. When you get home,
be careful where you look for dreams." Waves
on the big lake agreed, crashing now and again
into the conversation. "You need to test the water
before jumping in." The sky was getting lighter.

"Let's check the tree-hung closet. Sometimes it's lighter
than a feather. Sometimes it's heavier than big shore
stones piled high along the water.
Something's in the closet for you to wear when you go home."
Again,
the girls wondered what they were getting into, but they waved

away the thought. Tina Christina's aunt waved
the three girls closer, unwinding twine around the tree. Lighter
than they had seen her, Aunt Tina sang the same song again
and over, eyes on the horizon across the shore.
The closet slid slowly down the trunk. Christina thought of home
and her own closet while Big Lake Water

settled down, clear as a mirror. Teapot's water
simmered on the fire. Waving
the three girls even closer, Aunt Tina said, "Home's
your beginning. Then you cross the threshold. Lighter
and much brighter, the far shore
will call you. Over and again."

Looking again at the far shore,
lighter than Aunt Tina's camp and unlike home,
they waved and walked into the closet, high above the water.

In the closet a small light flickered before
it burst into a flame and called their names.
"Girls,
you've seen the sights these summer
nights. Next time, put on your sandals and your capes
when you awaken in your dreams. You'll

see that you'll..."
The light went out. Before
them, the girls saw three capes
escape from the closet lining. Their names
floated eerily above them like summer
fog, thrilling the three girls.

"Wrap up in your capes, girls,"
said the voice. "Then you'll
be free to fly." The capes, like summer
breezes, wrapped themselves around the girls before
they reached into the air. Their names
sparked like fireworks, spangling their capes.

Recently escaped, these capes
were cashmere in each girl's
favorite color. "Three times say your names,"
said the voice, "and you'll
find before
you three pairs of summer

sandals. Your summer
soles will fly across the dark. Put on your capes
and levitate." Before
they knew it, the girls
rose as a triangle and slipped into their sandals. "You'll
need to raise one hand to land," said the name-

less voice to the name-
sake girl and her companions. No summer
light filtered into the birchbark closet. "You
must reverse your capes
to see the shores of Big Lake Water." The fame-game girls
felt in the dark once more as they often had before.

Capes and sandals held before them, the three girls
left Aunt Tina's summer closet, but you'll
know by now the way the sisters came they could not name.

*A*unt Tina smiled at the two bewildered girls,
"Now you know about the wild life –
capes
and sandals, deep creek dreams,
and guides like Great Horned Owl.
It's time for you to follow the stacked stones back home."

The sisters, striking out for home
with Christina, took the lead. "Goodbye," called the three girls
to Aunt Tina as Owl
flew overhead and hooted, "Life
at home won't always be a dream."
The capes

reversed themselves and flew around the three. Wrapped in capes,
they rose in a triangle and sailed across the sky. Home
materialized: A cairn on the horizon. Dreaming
themselves awake, the girls
were dazzled by the night's still life
of stars. In the silence, Great Horned Owl

could still be heard, although Owl
no longer was in sight. The landscape
grew familiar before they realized their lives
would never be the same. "We're almost home,"
said Christina. The three girls
raised their hands to land. The sisters didn't dream

their trip would be anything like this. Their daydreams
might have had an owl
but not a Martian teapot or Mr. Moon Man with three girls
on his trapeze. They tiptoed in their capes
and sandals into Christina's home,
where there was no sign of life

at this late hour. Their life
before their visit to Aunt Tina seemed forgotten as their dreams
flew home,
quiet as a great horned owl,
and pressed themselves upon the capes
of the three girls.

No longer night owls, the three girls hung their dream capes
in Christina's closet before the sisters cried, "We're home!
Enough of scarves and pearls, we want the wild life!"

Biographies

Tina Christina Sestina is Susan Hawkinson's first illustrated book, written for both adults and children. She also is the author of *Timber Connections: The Joyce Lumber Story*, a Minnesota book award finalist. She lives in northern Minnesota. For presentations, book signings, and book purchases, contact her at **susanondoan@gmail.com**.

Anna Cain is the illustrator of this book and lives in South Minneapolis. *Tina Christina Sestina* is her first collaboration with an author. The medium for her illustrations is scratchboard. Using a sharp blade, Anna scratches away the black surface to reveal the image. Contact her at **annacain@gmail.com**.

Krista Matison is a graphic designer and artist in Grand Rapids, Minnesota. Her design work is an extension of her art. To see samples of her work or to contact her, go to **kristamatison.com**.